More Advance Praise for

# LOVE LOUDER:

"Preston Smiles is one of the true emerging leaders of our time. He carries a vision of a sacred world and inspires others to take action to manifest it."

—Dr. Michael Bernard Beckwith

"Preston Smiles is unstoppable! His passion and unique way of making the complicated simple make *Love Louder* a gift for any reader who wants practical tools for taking on life's daily challenges."

—Jack Canfield, author of the #1 *New York Times* bestselling *Chicken Soup for the Soul*® series and *The Success Principles*™

"Preston Smiles slaps you in the face with life's forgotten truths. His infectious energy leaves you feeling refreshed and awakened to your own path of possibility. While fully invoking his masculinity, it is his caring, sensitive, and loving nature that makes him a true man and a hero to many. I am blessed to call Preston a friend."

—Britt Hysen, founder of *Millennial Magazine*

# LOVE

## 33 Ways to

# LOUDER

## AMPLIFY YOUR LIFE

### PRESTON SMILES

WITHDRAWN

NORTH STAR WAY

New York   London   Toronto   Sydney   New Delhi

NORTH
STAR
WAY

North Star Way
An Imprint of Simon & Schuster, Inc.
1230 Avenue of the Americas
New York, NY 10020

First North Star Way paperback edition June 2016

NORTH STAR WAY and colophon are trademarks of Simon & Schuster, Inc.

For information about special discounts for bulk purchases, please contact Simon & Schuster Special Sales at 1-866-506-1949 or business@simonandschuster.com.

The North Star Way Speakers Bureau can bring authors to your live event. For more information or to book an event contact the North Star Way Speakers Bureau at 1-212-698-8888 or visit our site, thenorthstarway.com.

Interior design by Davina Mock-Maniscalco

Manufactured in the United States of America

10   9   8   7   6   5   4   3   2   1

Library of Congress Cataloging-in-Publication Data

Names: Smiles, Preston, author.
Title: Love louder : 33 ways to amplify your life / by Preston Smiles.
Description: New York, NY : North Star Way, 2016.
Identifiers: LCCN 2015049277 | ISBN 9781501120145 (paperback)
Subjects: LCSH: Conduct of life. | Self-realization. | Love. | BISAC:
   SELF-HELP / Personal Growth / Happiness. | SELF-HELP / Motivational &
   Inspirational. | SELF-HELP / Personal Growth / Self-Esteem.
Classification: LCC BJ1589 .S645 2016 | DDC 158--dc23
LC record available at http://lccn.loc.gov/2015049277

ISBN 9781501120145
ISBN 9781501120152 (ebook)

*This book is dedicated
to my amazing Queen Alexi Panos
for her ceaseless love and dedication to life.*

*For my mother, Jackie; father, Preston; sister, Shalea;
and all of my immediate and distant family.*

*To all my spiritual teachers,
who include all the saints and sages of all religions,
every bully that I fought, every coach, principal, mentor,
and counselor who believed in me,
all the Love Mobbers, and all the amazing people
whom I've encountered along my journey.*

# Contents

# Introduction

Do you find yourself feeling overwhelmed and stressed out more often than you'd like to admit? Being stalked by your inner critic, the one constantly telling you you're not good enough? Have you been waiting for your life to take off, but have no clue how to make that happen? Well, you're not alone; in fact, many people feel the same way. We've gotten so caught up buying the newest gadgets, keeping up with our Facebook and Instagram accounts, and paying the bills that we've lost our way. If you're ready to take your life to the next level, then you've found the perfect book, or the perfect book has found you. You see, I don't believe in mistakes. I believe that when the student is ready, the teacher will appear, and that sometimes following your heart means losing your mind. It means letting go of what's logical and moving into the unknown, or at least that which goes against what you've been taught.

In *Love Louder,* you will learn how to radically embrace life, breaking through personal barriers and moving forward with confidence and passion. This book was written to help you get out of your own way and live the life you're meant to live. It's comprised of thirty-three timeless tools that have supported thousands of people in regaining their center and getting what life is all about: love. I like to think of these wisdom nuggets as guideposts or flashing lights on a dark night, leading you home . . . to you.

You will get maximum value out of *Love Louder* if you stay out of a right-or-wrong, agree-or-disagree attitude and simply try things on as they pertain to your life. And don't feel that you have to read this chronologically. Keep it with you, read a chapter, and work on that lesson for a week. Think of it as a toolbox at your disposal, to continually crack open and apply. The only thing I strongly warn against is just racing through this, trying to consume another self-help book. I challenge you to apply everything that you read to your own life and see for yourself whether these tools work.

I wrote this book because I had to. I know firsthand what it feels like to feel lost, stressed, and overwhelmed by life. Over the last ten years I've been on a mission to discover and uncover what creates lasting happiness in humans. In that time, I've traveled all over the world immersing myself in ancient wisdom and applying it to my life.

I learned through countless workshops, thousands of books, hundreds of flights all over the world, that no matter what the question is, LOVE is the answer. Without a shadow of a doubt, I know that when you amplify your love, you automatically amplify your life. Loving louder is about answering that inner call, no matter how weird, obscure, or off the beaten path it may seem. Each of us was made *on* purpose, *with* a purpose, and it's our duty to get out of our own way to fulfill that which is burning in our hearts.

# Things WON'T CHANGE unless you do.

# 1

# LET GO AND TAKE THE RIDE:
## THE POWER OF TRUSTING THE JOURNEY

*Trust your dreams, your heart, and the journey of life . . . even when you don't understand it.*

Some people get so caught up in the destination that they miss that life is about the journey. They're so focused on the finish line that they miss that the beauty is in what and who you become on the way to the destination. I've received so many blessings in disguise in the form of health scares, people passing away, breakups, breakdowns, and so much more; and the thing that has supported me most is *trusting in the journey*. There is always more than meets the eye in every situation; and when we trust and have faith that all is well, even when it doesn't appear to be, we open ourselves up to new possibilities that we can apply in our lives.

When we trust the journey of life, wholly and completely, we don't need to know what is unfolding or why; we simply need to be present to the experience of it. Trusting the journey means that even if we don't understand what's unfolding right now, we have an unshakable belief that it's happening because circumstances are rearranging themselves for our highest good. It means knowing that for every door that closes, a window of opportunity opens. I've noticed that many people get so down about the front door's slamming in their face that they miss the open window and the back door that swung open at the same time.

**Ever** *since my house* **burnt down,** *I see the moon more clearly.*
—from the movie *Ashes and Snow*

Sometimes it's not until we've had it all taken away that we truly understand what it means to have faith. In those moments, standing metaphorically naked and vulnerable, we're forced to surrender to what is so that we can allow the journey to unfold as it needs to. Sometimes certain people or circumstances aren't meant for our lives, and we often don't realize it until we look back, years later. When we trust the journey, we can rest assured that every breakdown is a catalyst for a breakthrough.

# #LoveLouderAffirmation

Today I am available for all the good that is happening right now, regardless of how it may appear.

# 2

# INTENTION

Intention is the beginning of every idea. Everything that's happening on the planet started with an intention. Whether you plan to go to the gym, call a friend, or scratch an itch, it all starts with an intention to do so.

The common misconception is that we can intend something and just sit back and wait for it to happen; that intention alone will bring us everything that we've ever wanted. Let's be clear: intention is not wishful, airy-fairy thinking, but rather like an arrow flying toward a target when we are clear and focused.

*Loving Louder* is about living a purpose-driven life, being intentional with our thoughts, words, and actions. When you live life intentionally, it's like planting seeds in a garden and tending them. Whatever you plant and nurture will eventually grow. Intention is the planting and your thoughts, words, and actions are the nurturing. We can't plant cherry seeds and expect an avocado tree, just as we can't plant the seeds of fear and expect love to magically appear in our lives.

For years I was blocking out love and restricting the good in my life because I was focusing on everything I *didn't* want to happen. I was planting seeds of self-doubt and criticism, then expecting my dreams to come true. I wanted to meet the love of my life and to be fulfilled in my career, but I wasn't cultivating that kind of garden. The garden I was working on was the garden of my biggest fears and worries. I was unknowingly spending my time watering, cultivating, and giving fear all of my attention and intention. No matter what I genuinely said I wanted, I continued to call in what my inner intention was focused on. We interrupt the manifestation process by worrying, waiting, or holding on to thoughts that contradict our true intention.

One way we do this is with our reticular activating system. Yes, this is technical sounding, but it's important. This system is like a filter between our conscious mind and our subconscious mind. It takes instructions from our conscious mind and passes them on to our subconscious, letting in all the relevant information that otherwise might've remained as background noise. For instance, have you ever noticed that when you're really hungry, you begin noticing restaurants, billboards, and ads about food? Or have you ever done research on a particular car and then all of a sudden you start seeing it everywhere? The billboards and cars have always been there, but now because of your reticular activating system, they come into your awareness more frequently.

On the other hand, have you ever been late, and everyone and everything seems to be going especially slow? All the traffic lights are red, and people seem to keep getting in your way. On the surface you may say that it wasn't your intention to be late, but we must remember that the universe is like a giant ball of Play-Doh molding to whatever thought we continue to hold on to and put action behind. In those moments, all you're focused on is how late you'll be, and so the infinite field of possibility and your reticular activating system kick into gear, fulfilling that request. Your unconscious is focused on being late, and therefore you're intentionally drawing more "late" into your life. This process is happening whether we're aware of it or not, and it takes directions based on whatever your attention is homing in on.

When we continue to focus on that which is positive in our life, our reticular activating system will show us more of the positive. Think of it as the arrow that joins with the bow, pointed toward a target; it will hit whatever you're focused on. If you desire love but you're in a constant state of fear and distrust, no matter how focused the arrow is on love, it will miss that target and hit the one you're spending all that time thinking about. Our intentions have to be crystal-clear and in alignment with our thoughts and actions in order for us to hit the target.

Here are four steps for harnessing the power of intention.

1. **Make it real for yourself.** Figure out what your intention is without BS'ing yourself. Saying you intend to have a million dollars tomorrow when you're making minimum wage and have no plan of action is not realistic and will cause your subconscious mind to go into doubt faster than a speeding bullet. So begin with small intentions to develop the muscle of manifestation through daily practice. Whether you're choosing an intention for the moment, such as "I intend to greet my coworkers with a smile," or you're choosing your in-

tention for the day, as in "I will take on this day with an attitude of gratitude," it has to be something that feels achievable.

2. **Schedule it.** Take five minutes in the morning to visualize what you want that day to be like and also what you desire your larger dream or goal to look like. Shut your eyes and let your imagination run wild, tasting, smelling, and feeling what it would feel like to already have achieved that desired result: giving that concert, running that marathon, receiving the Oscar, or meeting the person of your dreams. Then throughout the day, set "intention alarms" in your phone as a reminder of what you intended that morning; as they go off, bring yourself back to the visualization you did and see yourself having what you desire. A visual reminder, like a vision board, is also helpful in keeping the dream alive and present in your conscious mind.

3. **Take action.** Intention cannot be reached through words and thoughts alone. It's like thinking you'll lose weight but never getting off the couch and then wondering why you haven't lost a pound. There's an old expression we used on the streets: "Don't talk about it, be about it." In other words, it's not real until you put movement behind it. Moving the intention into action magnifies

the power of the intention and creates momentum and movement toward making it a reality.

4. **Sharing is caring.** Make your intentions known by sharing them with like-minded supporters. The point of this is twofold: when you share your vision with others, it strengthens and builds forward momentum and it makes you instantly accountable for what you've shared.

Whether your intention is about something in the near future or something that may take years, stay focused and stay in action toward that vision. Visualizing, writing, sharing, and putting action behind it will gather all the forces of the universe to support its manifestation.

# #LoveLouderChallenge

Set an intention with one or all of these below.

Today I stand for . . .

Today I choose to be . . .

Today I am a possibility for . . .

Today I am a demonstration of . . .

Today I am committed to . . .

# 3

# GRATITUDE

*H*ave you ever noticed how many people are searching for happiness, as if it's this elusive thing that's always "out there"? We've been conditioned to think that it's outside of us, in things, accomplishments, and goals. We say stuff like "If only I could get a better job, lose more weight, or make more money, THEN I would take the vacation, look, and feel better." Some people prefer the *Why?* game, asking themselves super disempowering questions like "Why do I always meet the taken ones?" "Why was I born into a poor family?"

"Why did so-and-so get that job over me even though I deserved it more?"

*Happiness* cannot be traveled to, owned, **earned**, worn or consumed. *Happiness* is the spiritual experience of **living every minute** with **love**, *grace*, and gratitude.

—Dennis Waitley

I travel to Tanzania every year to build clean water wells with my wife's organization E.P.I.C. (Everyday People Initiating Change). Recently we met a little girl named Upendo; her name means *love* in Swahili. She has a rare degenerative skin disease, along with skin cancer, which is eating away her entire face and body. When we met her, at an orphanage, the doctors gave her just enough morphine to make her comfortable as she was dying. This little girl was the most present and loving eight-year-old I've ever met. Her appreciation for life spilled into our hearts as she sang us song after song through her bandages, which were wrapped around her entire head like a mummy, with only one of her eyes and her mouth visible. Although she was dying, Upendo was full of joy and light, teaching us all the true meaning of gratitude and a wealthy spirit.

The wealthiest people on the planet are not just those who have millions in their bank account, although that doesn't hurt; no, the wealthiest people on the planet are those who are grateful for what they do have. Your outlook determines your outcome, and your outlook is determined by the amount of gratitude you practice.

Practicing gratitude is easy when everything is going according to plan, but can you be grateful in the midst of a breakup? Can you be grateful while you are taking care of a sick parent or child, or when everything seems to be imploding? I've found that no matter how tough life seems at the moment, there is always something to be grateful for. We get caught up in the glass's being half empty or half full, but the challenge is to be grateful that we *have* a glass. Good, bad, or ugly . . . you are blessed because you have LIFE. We cultivate gratitude by what we choose to focus on. When you stop focusing on what you think you need to be happy and practice being thankful for what you already have, you automatically tap into the abundance of life.

I share Upendo's story to remind us all that happiness does not come from circumstances. *Happiness comes from being grateful for what is, no matter what it may look like.* Giving thanks for all you've been given is the gas that life is powered by. Dance, live, sleep, and speak in gratitude. Make it a place you visit as much as possible, acknowledging all you've been blessed with. Most people are concerned with getting through the day, but gratitude is about what you can get from the day.

# #LoveLouderChallenge

Stop right now and notice your breath; notice the feeling of life moving through you with each passing breath. Look around you and recognize, with a grateful heart, the colors, shapes, sounds, and smells that fill that space. Notice details: a tree swaying in the wind, the chatter from the people next to you at the café, the texture of your office cubicle, and the smell of fresh-brewed coffee.

Begin to feel grateful for the gift of sight, the miracle of hearing, and the beauty of all your other senses; be astonished by how your brain works. Life is constantly emerging all around you, and how beautiful is it that you get to experience it fully?

We get in Life **WHAT WE GIVE** *TO* *LIFE*.

# 4
# The Key to Living Is Giving

*g*iving is a selfish act. You can't give to another without giving to yourself first.

Shakespeare reminds us about the power of giving in *Romeo and Juliet* when Juliet says:

> *My bounty is as boundless as the sea,*
> *My love as deep; the more I give to thee,*
> *The more I have, for both are infinite.*

Shakespeare was pointing out the universal law of circulation, or what I like to call the *double boomerang effect*, where you throw from one hand and receive someone else's throw in the other. This principle is how you're reading this book right now. I'm part of a group called the Association of Transformational Leaders, which was started by Mr. Jack Canfield, author of the hugely successful Chicken Soup for the Soul series. When I was accepted, I got a call from the man who nominated me, Freeman Michaels, the host of *Cutting Edge Consciousness*. He congratulated me and then let me know that I needn't look any further, that everything I would need will be within ATL.

A few weeks later I found myself at the retreat having a blast, and on the last day I walked into a packed dining area. I experienced that panicky feeling from the first day of junior high: Where do I sit when I don't quite know anybody? Here I was, at this fork in the road, staring at all the "cool" kids sitting and laughing over to my left, and then over to my right, a man sitting alone. It was kind of like that scene in *Home Alone* when Macaulay Culkin slaps his face; I was stuck. But in a moment of clarity I chose to take the opportunity to share time with someone and give the gift of company. As we began to talk, I realized that I chose to sit next to Bruce Cryer, the former CEO of the HeartMath Institute. We shared stories and laughed our butts off about life and its many facets. Bruce and I exchanged information and vowed we'd hang again.

About three months later, Bruce introduced me to my now publisher and the rest is history.

There is no possible way I could've orchestrated something that elaborate on my own. But because I was focused on giving, an unexpected boomerang came my way. The key to living is giving, and I urge you to give your gifts away, coming from service. Look for ways to add value to everyone you encounter in life, and indirectly your cup will be filled (and you'll feel pretty amazing in the process).

# #LoveLouderChallenge

In the next twenty-four hours, find a creative way to give to one person without using money. It could be a compliment, a shoulder to lean on, an ear to listen, a good laugh, or a secret love note.

# 5

# From a Seed to a Tree:

## Growing Gains

*C*hange is mandatory, but choosing personal growth is optional.

A key component to loving louder is choosing personal growth as a conscious practice. It's my belief that we're either moving forward or moving backward, but we're never *not* moving even when we feel stuck. The idea is to choose growth consciously so that we may keep moving forward and reach our fullest potential.

Personal growth is a process of understanding and developing oneself to be used as a vessel for love. Similar to going to the gym and lifting weights to grow our muscles, being committed to growth is about going into the inner gym to develop a foundation of emotional, intellectual, and spiritual fortitude. It's about pushing out to the edge of the metaphorical cliff, looking out into the unknown, and jumping off. It's about honoring what is while being inspired by what's in the way. Seeking out all the places where you're still playing small, holding back, and operating from fear.

I find that a lot of people are addicted to their comfort zone, and that's just fine, but nothing ever grows there. Comfort zones are like overgrown gardens, where we'd probably find a bunch of rocks, weeds, and debris from the area not being tended to. The soil would need to be cleaned and tended to if you want it as beautiful and healthy as possible. Similarly, old philosophies, attitudes, and habits must be cleared out if you want to plant the seed of an extraordinary life.

Your history does not determine your destiny. Your destiny is determined by your willingness to face yourself, push past your comfort zone, and grow. Be the rose in the concrete, the one who chooses growth no matter the circumstances. This means choosing to let go of the excuses and blame: "He hurt me," "I'm not ready yet," "I'm too old," "I'm too young," or any other excuse your ego can concoct.

Once this process is under way, the possible results are endless. You will be in the process of using your full potential to benefit yourself and others. New skills and talents will be discovered. Old relationships will be strengthened and new ones will emerge. The more we step out of our comfort zone, the more we build on other zones of life that we can enjoy living in.

We're all individuals, so there are no one-size-fits-all ways to go about this, but below are a few questions that are an excellent place to begin:

## Where are you currently?

Take a look at your strengths and challenge points as well as the habits that do and don't serve you.

## Where would you like to be?

Take a look at what you'd like to improve about yourself and why you want to improve those things. So, say, if you'd like to lose weight, specify how much weight and why you want to lose it.

## What's the vehicle that will support that? What do you need?

Determine what knowledge you need to have and the experiences that must happen in order for you to get closer to your desired self. Find resources useful toward achieving this desired state, resources that aid in the growth and development of social, emotional, intellectual, and spiritual traits.

## What is a feasible timeline?

Make a list of activities and events you hope to experience within a set amount of time. Use them as checkpoints in moving toward your goal.

Small hinges SWING BIG DOORS. Small steps daily LEAD TO BIG OPPORTUNITIES. ROME WASN'T BUILT IN A DAY AND NEITHER WILL YOUR DREAMS BE ACHIEVED THAT QUICKLY, but when you focus on SMALL DAILY ACTIONS, you open yourself up to BIG POSSIBILITIES.

# 6

# The "F" Word!

## Forgiveness

There is no enemy more fierce, harsh, and utterly ruthless than the one living inside our own heads. We hold ourselves in mental and emotional prisons for years, over something we've done or something that has been done to us. Tapping into the practice of forgiveness is powerful medicine for the journey of self-love and healing. We all make mistakes. If you're living, it's inevitable that you're going to do something dumb. The key to loving louder is forgiving yourself and those who may have hurt you. Holding on to pain and being resentful does more damage to you than it does to the person you're aiming it at.

> *It takes* **courage** *to forgive those who may have* **harmed us,** *but we don't forgive people because we're* **weak,** *we forgive because we're* **compassionate** *enough to know that we all make* **mistakes.**

I was sixteen when I hopped in the car with some friends to go on what I thought was just a joyride to West Hollywood. Until we got to the grocery store nearby, I was unaware that the plan was to egg gay men walking on Santa Monica Boulevard, the epicenter of the gay community. As my friends joked about how much fun it was going to be, I had an unsettled feeling in my stomach.

As we approached the first group of men who were holding hands, my friends pulled up slowly and howled "Faggots!" out the window while hurling eggs like baseballs. As the eggs crashed on the store windows behind them and the guys ducked and ran off, my friends sped off, laughing hysterically. As we approached a red light, one of them commented that I didn't throw any. "Nah, man, I couldn't get my hand out the window," I sheepishly explained. As we drove home, I felt a deep sadness for what I had taken part in, something that I would bury deep within me out of shame.

Six years later, as a part of my graduate school program, I was cast in *The Laramie Project,* a play about a gay college student named Matthew Shepard who was brutally killed because of his sexuality. As rehearsals began, I felt an undeniable guilt. Over the next couple of weeks, as I stepped further into my character's role, I became noticeably quiet and withdrawn. Things got worse for me when I discovered that, during rehearsals, a young man in the town where I was attending school had been sodomized and burned to death because he was gay. After his brutal death, his best friend Christine came to talk to the cast of the play about how important this subject truly was.

Flash-forward to opening night. The theater was completely packed. As the lights went up on the stage, I stepped out to deliver my opening lines; directly in my field of view was Christine. As if a gigantic anvil had been dropped on me, I felt the weight of all that I had done, the pain of Matthew Shepard, the guilt of the men who did that to him, and everyone else who had been attacked because of whom they loved. I instantly burst into tears. I couldn't say a word. I was a puddle, completely stopping the show with overwhelming guilt for what I was part of in my teenage years. As one of the actors escorted me off the stage, I flashed back to that night years ago in Hollywood, realizing that I had been punishing myself ever since.

I regained my composure enough to finish the show, but afterward I spoke with my best friend about it and began the process of forgiving myself. Two months later, after the play's run was over, I realized how deep my guilt went and how much love I was withholding from myself and others. Now, almost twenty years later, I know that my life took a drastic turn when I forgave myself. Through the process of self-forgiveness, I opened up a physical and emotional space in my heart that I could now share with the world. I gained a new sense of compassion for myself for not speaking up, as well as for the other kids who took part that night, for they were acting out what pain they felt internally. Over the years I've become increasingly aware that those in the most pain tend to cause it for others, and instead of judging and punishing them, we should offer love and compassion. As *A Course in Miracles* states, "All attack is a cry for help." And most important, I gained an unwavering knowing that love is love, and judgments have no place in my heart.

Forgiveness can be hard when you are dealing with deep injustices from others. It may be hard to give mercy to someone who didn't give mercy to you, but know that it is all a process. If you find that you get uncontrollably angry when thinking about a particular situation or person, that's perfectly fine, as we all have our own timelines. Forgiveness is a journey that takes time and effort, so don't condemn yourself for feeling what you feel. Rest assured that as you begin the process of forgiveness, the thoughts of revenge and anger will eventually change into thoughts of love and compassion. The more you open up your heart to compassion, the more you begin to realize that most injustices come from a place of hurt within the wrongdoer and the only way to heal it is with love. Most of the pain I caused others as a teenager was because of the inner pain I was feeling.

Forgiveness doesn't excuse what happened; it prevents what happened from destroying your heart.

Hurt people *hurt* people.

THAT'S HOW PAIN PATTERNS GET PASSED ON, GENERATION AFTER GENERATION AFTER GENERATION.

Break the chain today.

Meet *anger* with *sympathy,*

CONTEMPT WITH COMPASSION,

*cruelty* with *kindness.*

Greet grimaces with smiles.

FORGIVE AND FORGET ABOUT FINDING FAULT.

*Love* is the WEAPON

of the *future.*

—Yehuda Berg

# #LoveLouderChallenge

Make a list of everything and everyone you haven't forgiven. It may look like this:

My second-grade teacher, for messing my name up over and over again

Myself, for cheating on my biology test in college

The government, for not having universal health care

The girl in the elevator in Las Vegas when I was ten who clowned me in front of my friends when I told her she was pretty

My grandfather, for not reaching out and wanting to know me earlier

Then choose one of the instances from your list and repeat this with love in your heart: "I forgive you for what you've done." Say it until you can truly understand it from a place of compassion. Remember, we all make mistakes and are all doing the best we can, reflecting our current level of consciousness.

# SURRENDER!

*Let go*

of the need to have

*it all figured out*

AND SURRENDER

TO WHAT IS.

# 7

# The Story of the Two Wolves

*There once was a Cherokee elder who was teaching his grandchildren about life. He drew the children around him one night as they sat by the campfire and looked around the circle and said solemnly, "There is a fight going on inside me. It's a terrible fight! And it's between two wolves. One wolf represents fear, anger, envy, sorrow, and resentment. The other wolf stands for joy, peace, love, hope, and kindness. This same fight is going on inside of you and every other person too."*

*The children sat wide-eyed in silence for a moment. Then one youngster asked, "But, Grandfather, which wolf will win?"*

*The old Cherokee paused and looked into his grandchild's eyes and replied after a short pause: "The one I feed."*

Which wolf are you feeding? If you're like most people, you would prefer to feed the wolf of love but are most likely feeding the wolf of fear. But don't fret, there's a scientific reason behind this.

According to scientists, we think about 50,000 to 70,000 thoughts a day. Most of them are the same thoughts we had the day before and the day before that. How crazy is that? We're like human loop machines, playing the same tracks over and over. The thing that really blows me away is that 80 percent of those thoughts are negative, or fear-based, in nature. How many times a day are you ambushed by thoughts about how you're not good enough, how you're bound to fail, or how you won't have enough money, time, or energy to do XYZ?

The average person's mind is geared toward the wolf of fear because we're hardwired, from caveman days, to pay more attention to potential threats than to positive thoughts. This negative bias goes back to early man's need to avoid being eaten by a predator. Paying attention to the negative is what allowed us to survive as a species. While we're not so concerned with giant creatures chasing us anymore, our brains are still predisposed to focus on fear. Which is why consciously choosing the wolf of love is highly important for your overall happiness and for the rewiring of your brain.

The best solution I've come up with involves using gratitude to turn negative thoughts into positive ones. So the moment a negative thought comes up, you redirect it to a thought about something you're grateful for. In doing this, we train the brain to look for the good in every situation and to not identify with the negative.

When we identify with the madness of our everyday thoughts, we set ourselves up for a life of sadness and anxiety. We must realize that our thoughts are not facts and that we always have a choice of what to focus on.

When we continue to focus on the good, we train our brains to think new, positive thoughts. In my experience, thoughts are like fishing: we're the fish, and the thoughts are the fisherman. A thought tosses out bait to see if you'll bite; if you take the bait, the thought takes you. But if you don't take the bait, the fisherman gets tired and goes fishing somewhere else. Your job is to be an observer of the thoughts and to choose consciously if you want to take that bait.

# #LoveLouderChallenge

Step one: be an observer of your thoughts this week. Pay attention to the patterns in your thoughts, those ideas that continuously come up. Then move on to step two, which is directing your thoughts to something that you *do* want to think about, thus consciously feeding the wolf of love. This is not about pretending you're a millionaire when you know you're broke; it's about finding a thought with a positive spin on it that feels true for you in the moment. Gratitude is the easiest place to start, because there is always something that you can be grateful for at any time, even if it's just being alive to experience it. So instead of feeding a thought like "I'm so broke, I can't pay my bills," we'll direct it to "I may not have all the money I would like to have right now, but I'm blessed to have the opportunity to create it."

# NIGHT IS COMING.

*It's not what happens,*

IT'S WHAT *you do* ABOUT WHAT HAPPENS.

## THE CHALLENGE IS TO

## DO *different* THINGS

with the **same** circumstances.

*You can't get rid of night,*

BUT YOU CAN BUY A BLANKET,

*go indoors, or start a fire.*

ARE YOU PREPARED?

# 8

# The Taste Test

*L*anguage has the power to transform. It's how we express our thoughts and feelings, but most people don't realize their *language* is a huge barrier to their freedom. Unless it's literally the end of the world (and it's not), you don't get to have a lifetime pity party. How we speak about things is a window into our view of reality.

Many of us have heard the phrase "change your thoughts, change your life." While this is a powerful bit of wisdom, it isn't always that easy to implement. In those tricky times when your life is feeling a little over-whelming, a change of language can be the gateway to changing your thoughts. By consistently replacing dis-empowering language with empowering language, we can transform our lives drastically.

The problem is, most of us have picked up our com-munication skills from the world we grew up in: from our parents, classmates, friends, and close family. If your mom was a complainer, as much as you swore you wouldn't be like her when you grew up, you most likely find it natural to lean toward negativity and complaining in life. If you grew up in a household of silver linings, you will be more inclined to find the good in everything. But don't fret. Every thought, statement, and feeling is creative in nature; therefore, we're always creating our current reality with the language we choose moment to moment. The idea here is to create by design, con-sciously choosing the language that leads to transform-ing our thoughts.

Most of the world, including me for most of my life, has no clue how the process of manifestation works. They're clueless as to how to design the life of their dreams, yet are unconsciously designing it in every wak-ing moment. Have you ever met someone who was "wronged" in some way or who has fallen on hard times and is obsessed with telling everyone? They have their story so fine-tuned that you could recite it back to them, almost word for word. That story is told over and over because they get a payoff every time they tell it: they get to be right about how messed up things are, they have a rationale for why their life isn't where it's supposed to be, and they get the sympathy of everyone around them. While that payoff may seem attractive to some, rest assured it's doing critical damage to what's possible for their future. Our thoughts and words create our reality by attracting into our lives more of what we're putting out into the world. The more we obsess about what's not working, the more things won't work. The more we use language of positivity and love, the more our energy will attract that into our space. My mom used to say, "If you don't have anything good to say, don't say anything at all," and now, twenty-five years later, I get that statement on a whole new level.

Bottom line, if you want your life to take off, you have to stop talking like a victim. So many of us are wishy-washy with our language, speaking from "I may," "I'll try," "I hope," and "I have to," instead of being definitive: "I WILL," "I CHOOSE TO," and "I DESIRE." Be conscious with your words—they make up your reality.

# YOU

ARE

*Loved.*

# 9

# Embrace the Breakdown:

## Turning Our Wounds into Wisdom

*I*n life there will be moments of pain and what seem to be insurmountable obstacles, but when you embrace those breakdowns, you can turn your wounds into wisdom.

I know it can be difficult to see anything other than the problem that you're facing when you're in the thick of it: repeatedly running worst-case scenarios in your head, holding on to the hurt, and focusing on what's not working. But the first step in turning your wounds into wisdom is switching your focus from what's not working to what *is*.

If we want to experience more love in our lives, there is no point in obsessing about the past and worrying ourselves to death over the negative. It takes the same amount of energy to wallow in the breakdown as it does to focus on the solution, so why not use our energy more productively? Yes, we learn from our mistakes, but most of our energy should be aimed toward what we desire. When we drive our energy in the direction of the solution, our thoughts, feelings, and actions begin to head that way.

Here are five ways to handle a breakdown:

1. Don't blame anyone outside of yourself, no matter how severe it is. If you're blaming, it stops the healing process and makes you a victim of whomever you're blaming.

2. Don't beat yourself up for feeling what you feel or doing what you did; it only makes things worse.

3. Don't overthink and analyze it. You'll drive yourself crazy. Instead, say out loud, "I accept this pain, for it is here to teach me something I need to know." Give yourself full permission

to experience whatever is coming up at that time. For example, if it's sadness and you feel a good cry coming on, don't bottle that up. Allow yourself to fully go there.

4. Don't try to numb the pain by distracting yourself with vices such as alcohol, drugs, television, people, or food. These are all temporary Band-Aids that will eventually come off, while the problem still remains.

5. After you've allowed yourself to fully experience the breakdown, figure out what you desire out of the situation and what that will take from you to achieve it. For example, if you went through a difficult breakup and you want to be at peace with it, you'll need to access the inner compassion and peace you have for the both of you. It may require that you remember some of the good times, forgive the bad, and begin to send him/her well-wishes.

Some of the most painful situations produce some of the most beautiful experiences. Every time I have felt rejection, I have also received direction. Every time I thought I couldn't go on, a miracle appeared.

The practice is to see the opportunity in the midst of the pain. Right in the middle of the situation—when you want to give up, when you want to retreat, when you want to dismiss it and blame others—is exactly when you have an opportunity to move into the beauty of it all. Let the pain be your teacher. Instead of having it break you, have it make you. Have the circumstances motivate and inspire you to look a little deeper and examine what's truly there. Don't waste the breakdown, don't waste the breakup, don't waste the anger; look into it, for it holds the key to your freedom. No matter what you're experiencing, know that it's the culmination of your thoughts, words, and actions up to this point, and you have the power at any given moment to shift it by shifting you.

PLA: Public Love Announcement

# RELATIONSHIP INSIGHT

Ladies, fellas, this is a public love announcement:

Please stop putting your hopes and dreams into one person. Nobody can handle that kind of pressure and it is not his or her duty.

I would go so far as to say, don't get into a relationship until you are clear that you're not doing it to fill a void within yourself. This is a friendly reminder that the love that you are is more than enough to fill up ten galaxies. You don't want to be in a dependent relationship, where someone has to be the dealer and someone the addict.

Make your partner the icing on the cake instead of the whole cake. That perspective is not only powerful but very attractive. I get that sometimes you meet someone and you just can't get enough; I have been there and in fact am still there. But we must treat our relationships like fine wine, giving them room to breathe so that we can taste all that they have to offer.

There is nothing more powerful than when two whole individuals come together and create a beautiful overlap that they get to share and experience together.

# 10

# How Does It Feel?

## What You Put In Is What You Get Out

There is nothing more important than how you feel. Those who have their health have everything.

Most people treat their car better than they do their own body, making sure it has the best gas, the engine is firing on all cylinders, and it's up-to-date on its tune-ups. If you put rocks in your gas tank instead of gas, your car won't last very long. Likewise, if you're eating unhealthy food, your body is bound to break down, or at the very least, not perform as well as it's capable of doing.

*Most people* don't *do* well *because* they don't **feel well.** **They don't** have *the* vitality to see their *dreams* through.

We all know that junk food doesn't do a body good. Unfortunately, what it usually takes for a shift to taking care of ourselves is a massive health scare. It's not until we know we're at the brink that we're willing to make radical shifts to save our lives. Loving louder includes loving our bodies enough to be proactive and fill our tanks with food that fuels us, instead of waiting for disaster to strike.

I was no exception to this. For all of my childhood and most of my adult life I have been addicted to fast foods, candy, and soda. So in 2005, after developing an irregular heartbeat and being given a prescription from a cardiologist, I decided to make some big changes fast. I cut out 99 percent of what I was eating and drinking and replaced it with healthier choices like green juices and more vegetables.

One of the biggest aha moments for me came after I made the shift in my habits. I realized that REAL food (not the processed junk I was used to eating) actually gives us energy after we eat. I no longer felt slow, bloated, lethargic, and fat, as I had in the past. It blew me away that after meals I felt alive and ready to take on the world instead of sleepy and slow. Other results of my eating healthy were that my skin started to look better, I woke up with an extra pep in my step, and overall I felt more alive than I ever had.

There is nothing more important than how we feel from moment to moment, and those momentary feelings are greatly influenced by the food we use to fuel our bodies. The body we come in with has an expiration date on it, but that doesn't mean it needs to be tired and barely alive when that day comes. We owe it to ourselves to consume things that give us energy, instead of processed junk that drains us.

*We cannot truly serve others until we first serve ourselves.*

# #LoveLouderChallenge

Be mindful of what you put in your body's "fuel tank" today. Before you put any food or drink in your mouth,

# You can HAVE IT All!

And by all _I_ mean your personal FREEDOM.

# 11

# Stop Trying to Make Everyone Happy

*H*i, *I'm Preston and I'm a recovering people pleaser.* People pleasing is a dangerous self-inflicted disease that kills dreams and sabotages relationships.

You're most likely suffering from people pleasing if:

1. You go out of your way to make other people happy at your own expense.

2. Your choices and actions are based on what others may think, want, or expect from you.

3. You constantly put others' needs ahead of your own.

4. You are always looking for ways to fit in.

People pleasers often hold back their true feelings because they don't want to offend others or rock the boat. They often find themselves in the position of mediator in the family or group of friends, catering to everyone, making sure everyone's needs are met, but often neglecting their own. Women in particular tend to have the "nurturing button" that eventually turns into people pleasing, ignoring self-care for the "good" of the family. If any of these scenarios fit you, you get to let that go and join the club of *recovering* people pleasers (like myself), those who know that when we take care of ourselves first, we're actually taking care of everyone else at the same time. We can't possibly give to others from our cup if we haven't been filling it first.

People pleasing can be debilitating, killing all of your hopes and dreams. In my workshops all over the world, I've met many people who have lived their entire lives based on what their parents want for them, not on what they want for themselves. But no matter how hard you try, you'll never (EVER) please everyone. I don't care how well intentioned you are, how loving you try to be, or how carefully you operate in life, YOU WILL NEVER PLEASE EVERYONE. It's a battle you simply can't win.

A part of loving louder is letting go of the need to take care of everyone else and focusing on what you want. You cannot turn the volume up on the amount of love you give to others until you are willing to turn it up first for yourself. You will constantly feel drained and anxious about getting your own needs met and therefore won't have the energy needed to truly share all of you with the world. Worse, you may even build up resentment for something YOU perpetuated. I learned this the hard way during my young adult years.

Someone close to me began a long struggle with drugs. Because he knew I was a people pleaser, he would come to me every week asking for small amounts of money. He would claim the funds were for necessities such as soap, toilet tissue, or food; but deep down, I knew the money was to feed his habit. No matter how much he made, he always found a way to bleed himself dry and come to old faithful (me!) for a re-up. Like clockwork, although everything in me wanted to say no, for ten long years I said yes.

It got all too real when I lent him my car to "get some food." A few hours later I got a call from the police saying that my car had been involved in a drug bust and I needed to get it from the police impound. Even then, after all of that, the guilt of our relationship kept me from saying no. The final straw came three years later, when we had a conversation in which I finally opened up about how I felt. He responded by saying that I was never there for him. I was outraged. After I had provided him with ten years of financial and emotional support, giving even when I didn't have it to give, he felt as though I had turned my back on him. While it stung to hear that, in that moment I truly understood that there was nothing I could do to save this person and that the resentment and pain were slowly killing me. I took ownership for how I had enabled his drug habit and decided enough was enough. Although I knew my distance could sever the relationship, I felt free and knew that I had begun the process of truly loving myself.

Here are three ways to begin your People Pleaser Recovery Program:

1. **When did you first notice it?** Take time to reflect on your first memories of people pleasing. Try to identify where your need to be a people pleaser came from, what hole you were attempting to fill. For me, the need for approval developed when I was nine years old after I was placed in special education classes. While my story may be unique to me, we all

have something—whether it was the praise we got every time we did something "right" as a child or the lack of praise—that caused us to search for approval or acceptance.

2. **Catch it in the moment.** Begin to cultivate a moment-to-moment awareness of when you are people pleasing. If you're like most of us, it's something you've been doing your entire life, so it may not be easy to spot at first. Certain people and scenarios trigger deeply ingrained habits, but if you look closely, you may see where you bend for the needs of others. Become aware of your patterns around making sure people like or approve of you. Catch yourself changing your shirt after someone comments on the color. Catch yourself staying silent when your uncle says something offensive. Catch yourself saying yes to a job that you clearly don't want to do, or giving that guy your number because you don't want to hurt his feelings.

   Also take stock of your mood after certain interactions. If you notice you're experiencing anger or feeling resentful, frustrated, or sad after you connect with someone, check in and see if you were people pleasing. Did you just say yes again to something you wanted to say no to? Did you lie to make someone happy or to keep him or her satisfied? Most of us have been people pleasing so long that we don't even notice we're doing it. Let your awareness of your feelings be an indicator for you; if you can begin to catch it, you can begin to correct it.

3. **Create healthy boundaries and practice keeping them.** We are what we continuously do. Whatever we habitually practice, we become skilled at. Reflect and journal about what matters to you. Write down what's okay for you and what's not okay for you. Write down what your deal breakers are, and what relationships are crossing those currently. Then begin to practice speaking up. Practice doing something that you may think of as small, like ordering something complicated at a restaurant, where you would usually not bother because you don't want to hold everyone up. Small steps lead to big change, so start finding small ways to reclaim your needs and desires.

The bottom line is that people pleasing is not a

healthy choice for any of us. For years I stressed myself and drained my energy trying to make sure everyone else's needs were taken care of, but that was a path that led me nowhere fast. There will always be someone who wishes you had done it some other way, always someone who just doesn't "do" you, and that's okay. It's not your job to please everyone. It's your job to do and be what makes you smile, to express yourself from the fullest version of you. If you are breathing, you will be judged. It's time we accept that and get on with OUR lives.

# #LoveLouderChallenge

Write a letter to someone you've been trying to please for a long time. In the letter, pour out all your feelings about him or her. Let the person know how it's felt trying to please him or her. Write down everything; don't stop until you get all of your thoughts and feelings on that paper. End the letter with how you intend to be from now on. When you feel complete, read it to someone you trust who is completely objective. After you have done this, tear the letter into little pieces. This process was for you, not for the person the letter was written to.

# 12

# Ask and It Is Given:

## The Art of Asking for Help

*B*ecause we live in a world that rewards the do-it-yourself, self-sufficient mentality, the idea of asking for help can be challenging at the least. But turning up the volume on your life requires mastering the art of asking for help. I used to view asking for help as a sign of weakness, but the truth was, I was really afraid of being rejected and looking bad. Meanwhile, year after year my career, relationships, and life remained the same. Things were changing, but I wasn't growing. It wasn't until I pushed past my fear and began asking others for help that my life began to take off.

I now know that it takes a massive amount of courage and vulnerability to ask for help, and that no matter what you desire on the planet, it involves people. We can't escape asking for support. And contrary to the bootstrapping do-it-yourself mentality being propagated around the world, we never ever do anything without the help of others.

*It's okay not to know everything.*

Instead of rearranging the deck chairs on the *Titanic,* we as leaders have to recognize that if we don't ask for help, our ship will sink. The key for us is to seek support from those who've accessed something we'd like to experience more of in our lives. In order to experience more joy and confidence, talk to, hang with, and ask for help from someone who is exhibiting those attributes on a consistent basis. If you'd like to make more money, ask someone who has demonstrated those skills consistently for support. You'll be surprised at how many people will not only be willing to but will go the extra mile to help you.

We all have a tribe of people who would love to be a shoulder to cry on, provide a warm hug, or impart a little advice. All you have to do is ask.

Here are three things you can do before asking for help.

1. **Admit that you need help.** This is big, because it often involves swallowing your pride and admitting that you aren't super(wo)man after all.

2. **Identify specifically what help you need.** The more detailed and clear you are, the easier it will be to help you.

3. **Identify who is skilled in that area.** Make a list of people you know and those you'd like to know. For example, authors, bloggers, business owners, couples, etc. Make sure you don't ask people who are not skilled in this area. For example, don't ask someone who's been single for years about how to create more passion in your relationship.

# 13

# Can You Hear Me Now?

One of the keys to loving louder is *listening* louder.

Stephen Covey, the author of *The 7 Habits of Highly Effective People,* wrote, "Seek first to understand, then to be understood." But some people do the exact opposite—hearing the words, but surely not listening. Some are just waiting to get their point across instead of genuinely being present. Take it from me, because for a very long time I didn't listen to other people; I was just waiting for them to finish, mentally reloading before I'd impart my opinion. The problem with this kind of communication is that very little listening is actually taking place.

To actively listen is to be present. Active listening is about being curious, engaged, and enthusiastic about what the other person is saying. It's about letting ourselves be moved and affected by what's being conveyed, without having to spout out our opinions or a rebuttal.

When you take the time to actively listen to someone, it's a special thing, because it's so rare. Listening is one of the highest forms of caring; it shows that you are truly there for someone and value what they have to say. When you give people your full attention—not waiting to talk, not reloading, not judging, but being fully present with them—you end up in an exchange that is ripe with possibility. Love louder by listening louder; you may be surprised at what you will learn.

# #LoveLouderChallenge

Ask someone you care about—a friend, coworker, or parent—the following question and set an intention to actively listen.

What was the happiest time of your life, and why? (If you ask your parents, tell them they can't say when you were born.)

### Four Keys to Active Listening

1. Breathe deep into the bottom of your belly.

2. Face the speaker, making eye contact (if he or she keeps turning away, don't take it personally; most people are not used to actually being listened to attentively).

3. Don't judge yourself if/when you check out. Active listening can be exhausting and takes practice.

4. Have fun and be you! Do your best not to think about YOU during this time; engage naturally, without being self-conscious.

# WHAT IF EVERYTHING
## IS PERFECT RIGHT NOW?
# TRUST THE TIMING
## of your life.

# 14

# Blue Frog Moments:

## Why You Should Pay Attention to What Pisses You Off

In my lifetime, I have been called a faggot, a nigger, a bi%@h, a punk, an a$$hole, a hypocrite, mean, closed off, and many other epithets. But only "closed off" really bothered me. Why?

Because some part of it was actually true. When I really thought about it, I was still guarding my heart and being selective with my love. A mentor of mine calls it a "blue frog" moment: if someone calls you a blue frog, you would laugh and not take it personally, because you know you're not an amphibian. But if that same person called you a liar, and it stings and cues up the defensiveness, bingo! That's where your work lies.

When I realized that being called "closed off" stung, I knew it was because it was true. I knew that I still had a lot of work to do in opening myself up, letting my guard down, and allowing people to see the real me. Now I use this tool all the time as a gauge to where there is still work to be done.

# #LoveLouderChallenge

Scan your life for those times when a comment toward you really ticked you off. Ask yourself if it was a blue frog moment. What lesson is in this for you? What did this trigger for you?

# 15

# TRUST YOUR INTUITION

*Intuition is the GPS for the soul.*

At some point we've all heard that small voice whispering guidance from within. "Kiss her now." "Turn left." "Don't get in that car!" "Take the deal." "Call your mom." "She's cheating on you." "Check on your friend." "Don't date that guy." These are all examples of signals that we get on a daily basis, whether we're tuned into them or not. Have you ever felt something was off about a situation but stayed in it anyway? Have you ever dated someone despite your gut warning you that it wasn't a good idea? What is that? And why is it that so many of us don't listen to it?

Most of us have been taught to look for answers outside of ourselves, but everything we need is already within, and it's called intuition. Our unconscious mind is a storehouse of hidden wisdom waiting to be harnessed. Trusting your intuition is about trusting yourself. The more you trust yourself, the more love you will have to give to yourself and to others.

I do my best to listen to my first thought, because my second, third, and fourth thoughts are usually the ones that talk me out of whatever my instinctual first answer was. This way of tuning in saved my life when I was fifteen. My best friend, Scott, called and asked me to come out and drink and hang, as we always did. But for some reason my gut said no. Although my reply had been a yes every other night, something deep within told me not to go. That night, everyone in that blue Astro van was shot, and Scott was killed. That decision to listen to my intuition saved my life.

Intuition isn't always a life-or-death thing; sometimes it's a matter of which line to pick at the supermarket or the discovery of a new route that avoids the traffic jam. Intuition can come through as a gut feeling, an aha moment, a body signal, or a flash of insight; it can unfold slowly like a movie or appear in a dream. It's usually subtle and appears differently for different people. But no matter how it comes, it can be one of the most powerful tools you have access to, when you choose to tune into it.

Although intuition is something we all have, we must exercise it to get the most value out of it. The following are four ways to help you activate your intuition and use it to love louder.

1. **Go within or you'll go without.** No matter what name we may give it, the wise inner voice inside us is always talking. The problem is, it's hard to hear over the mental chatter. Most people have an overactive mind and over-identify with their thoughts, which they mistakenly believe define—or are—them. We are so much more than our thoughts, and once you can learn to quiet the mental chatter, you can access your intuitive intelligence. I recommend twenty minutes a day of quiet time when you turn off the computer and the phone, shut the door, and just listen. Then take a few deep, slow breaths to relax your body. Focus your attention on inhaling and exhaling. When thoughts come, picture them as clouds floating by in the sky and sim-

ply watch them. Then refocus on your breath. You can call this meditation if you want to, but it's ultimately just a cool way of quieting your mind.

2. **Take action on all aha moments.** When you hear the call, answer. When you pay attention and act on your intuitive hits, you'll get more and more intuitive impulses. Intuition is activated when you trust it. The more you build your trust in it, the more results you'll begin to see. So whether you're in a conversation with someone and a flash of inspiration within says, "Offer to hug them," or you're walking down a street and you get a bad feeling in your gut, listen to it, trust it, and act on it. These moments can be awesome guides once you learn to trust them.

3. **Question and journal.** Don't be afraid to ask questions and wait for the answer. Be active in your communication, asking questions and making it a habit to listen and write down the answers. The communication is sometimes quick and subtle. Set aside five to ten minutes to still your mind. Present a question to yourself, such as "Is this the right time to take

that trip?" And then stay open to any sensations, flashes, or impressions you receive. If your gut feels good about it, go forward. If it's not sitting well with you or you're not clear, don't do it or move forward with caution.

4. **Listen to your body.** Your body has its own wisdom, catching everything and sending you signals all along the way. Notice which people give you energy and which people drain you. Use the body's signals to create a power team of energy givers, and begin to limit your time with the energy vampires and toxic people.

If you can't see the

# POSSIBILITY,

YOU'RE NOT LOOKING HARD ENOUGH.

There is an opportunity

CAREFULLY PLACED WITHIN EVERY TOUGH SITUATION.

# 16

# When Shift Hits the Fan:

## How to Shift into Neutral

All events are neutral events.

It's our interpretation of them that makes them "good" or "bad," "right" or "wrong." A key component to loving louder is shifting into neutral as much as possible and seeing the world from the lens of possibility. Just as when a car is in neutral it has an option to move forward, reverse, or remain where it is, we too can view life from a neutral and unattached space, leaving us with endless possibilities

One of the things that astonishes me about us humans is how many interpretations we can have of any given moment. I surf a lot, and the other morning I witnessed two guys yelling at each other over a wave. The first guy believed that the second guy was not supposed to be on the wave when he was. The second guy was upset with the first guy for disrespecting him by yelling at him. The event was neutral until guy number one positioned himself as the judge of what's right in the water. It was also still neutral until guy number two chose to see guy one's reaction as disrespectful. If either one of them had shifted into neutral, they would've seen that neither party meant any harm and that there were numerous options on how the interaction could've been handled. In no way am I saying that you need to be 100 percent neutral at all times, but cultivating a practice of STARTING in neutral—as opposed to starting in defense, anger, or judgment—will give you more perspective on the situation at hand.

Another way to describe living in neutral would be mindfulness, which is the practice of observing your life from a nonjudgmental, compassionate, and accepting attitude. Mindfulness begins with a simple awareness, paying attention to your experience from moment to moment. When I shifted into neutral and began practicing mindfulness, I saw that my emotions, thoughts, feelings, and body sensations were transitory. The things I thought were so important no longer held so much weight in my life. They would come and go almost like the evening breeze.

Rather than operating on automatic, reacting to negative thoughts, and swimming in your emotions, you should try to observe everything from a neutral point of view. Living from this kind of mindful awareness will immediately help you make wiser choices. And those wiser choices will have an effect on everything from your bank account and professional goals to your relationship with friends and family. Make the shift today.

# #LoveLouderChallenge

Pinpoint a situation or person in your life that you have a hard time with. Examples could be a coworker who takes your pens without asking, your mother's asking you about your relationship, or the traffic on a certain street or highway. I challenge you for one day to shift into neutral about that person or circumstance. If it's a person, reach out and speak to him or her from a neutral space, making it clear what you'd prefer moving forward. If it's the traffic you encounter, you get to choose an interpretation that lifts and propels you to be positive instead of frustrated. (For example, "Wow, there is so much traffic that I can now make those phone calls I've been neglecting to make.")

# 17

# GET OFF THE FENCE AND JUMP! GO HARD OR GO HOME!

All the best fruit is out there on the skinny branches.

Those who go big, risking it all, open themselves up to the possibility of gaining it all. Those who sit on the sidelines, commenting on those who are risking it all, are destined to live a life of what-ifs. Loving louder is about risking louder. When we want to turn the volume up on our lives, we have to know that there is great risk that comes with the territory.

My greatest fear is leaving this life knowing that I had more gas in my tank. When I pass away, I want to know that I left it all out on field: failing, falling, laughing, loving, crying, and everything in between. If we never take the risk, we'll never know what we're capable of. We all have dreams; we all have something that is calling our name, beckoning us forward. Loving louder is about recognizing that voice . . . and acting on it. It's about giving up the safety of the herd and pushing into the unknown zone, where dreams can become a reality.

Name a person who's accomplished something great, and you'll find a trail of risk along their personal path to greatness. Do you think Martin Luther King, Jr., wasn't afraid? Do you suppose that JFK, Mother Teresa, Gandhi, and Nelson Mandela weren't scared about how their message would be received? These were people who heard the call, felt the fear, and moved forward regardless. They weren't afraid to turn the volume up on their lives so they could ultimately turn the volume up on their love. When you're going after anything worthwhile in life, know that you're going to eventually fall, look stupid, and make mistakes; it's part of the process of achieving. If you're not failing, you're probably not stretching yourself. The comfort zone is a place where dreams go to die, and where vitality goes to die with it.

Can you RISK more than what you think is safe? Can you CARE more than you think is wise? DREAM more than what you think is practical? And EXPECT more than you think is possible? Put yourself out there. What imprisons you also points to your freedom; do that thing that you've been afraid of, and you will open yourself up to that feeling of freedom. No matter how it turns out, when you truly risk, you build a muscle inside that helps you reach a little further next time.

This is your moment; own it. If you're going to fall, fall forward, going after your dreams. The destination will always change, but the person you become on the way is priceless.

# #LoveLouderChallenge

What's the one thing you've been afraid to do or say for years? DON'T DIE WONDERING WHAT-IF. Do it NOW. Take one action toward that thing *right now*. Make the call, write the first page of that script, send the email to that person, tell her you love her, and so forth. Do it now . . . seriously.

IF YOU BUILD *YOU*,

THEY WILL COME.

*The best project*

YOU'LL EVER WORK ON IS

*YOU.*

# 18

# Leasing with an Option to Buy:

## Ownership

*We can learn a lot from our mistakes if
we weren't so busy denying them.*

Until we take full responsibility for ourselves and our actions, we're leasing our lives with an option to buy.

To love louder, we must release ALL excuses and take *ownership*—acknowledging and accepting the choices we've made and the consequences of those choices. Although we can't control all circumstances, we can control how we view our part in them. One of the most powerful questions we can ask ourselves is: How did I cause or allow this? As long as we're blaming anyone or anything for our current circumstances, we're in victim mode, and whoever or whatever we're blaming has our power.

The **content** of our *life*
will *not* change until
**we change** the *context*
of *our* life.

As I mentioned earlier in this book, I had a pretty big health scare with my heart in 2005, but what I didn't mention is how upset I was after hearing from my doctor that what I had been consuming for twenty-five years was not good for me. At first I lashed out and blamed the government, my family, my environment, the school system, and anyone else I could find to make accountable for my situation. However, after I realized that a few weeks of finger-pointing got me nowhere, I knew something had to shift. I shifted from my victim mentality of blaming everyone else for my heart condition to looking at all the choices I made or didn't make to cause it. And you know what? I felt a huge sense of power immediately return to my life. I was no longer a victim of my circumstances, and now I could DO SOMETHING about them. My context changed, and thus the content of my life changed. I began making healthier lifestyle choices and the heart palpitations went away, and I began experiencing more energy and a zest for life.

Whatever you're currently experiencing in life is based on you and nothing else. Your decisions can generate either great rewards or unwanted consequences. You can be the problem or you can be the solution; the difference is the choice to take complete responsibility for your life.

# #LoveLouderChallenge

Identify an area of your life that you're not happy with and write down three ways you caused it to happen or allowed it into your life. For example, I took responsibility for my bad eating habits and for waiting months until I finally went to see my doctor. I also could've researched the foods I had been consuming for years. I had to come to grips with the fact that I caused the palpitations. So if you went through a breakup, instead of blaming your ex, ask yourself what you were pretending not to know. What did you see and allow for months, maybe years, before it all exploded? Get it? Take your power back by taking responsibility.

Then write one action step you're committed to completing within a week to begin the process of taking ownership in that area. In my case, I stopped eating fast food. In the case of a breakup, you could write a letter of apology, explaining the part you played in the way things turned out.

# 19
# Attention Goes Where Energy Flows:
## Focus-Pocus

*W*here your attention goes, energy flows. This means that what you focus on, you give life to. Your thoughts and feelings are literally a magnet, attracting to you what you put your attention on. If you want to emanate and attract love in your life, focusing on and looking for love will inevitably bring more of it to you.

This principle applies to everything, even the things

we least want to happen. For example, if you really want to achieve something, but you're afraid of failing or messing it up, you'll likely attract the very thing you don't want to happen, because THAT'S what you're focused on. But don't fret, because focus also works to our advantage: no matter what negativity you're experiencing, if you shift your thoughts, words, and actions toward the positive, you'll attract more of that. Energy is neutral; it goes where you direct it. Therefore you get what you focus on.

For years I struggled as an actor in LA. I was walking into audition rooms afraid of not getting the job and not knowing where my next paycheck was coming from. I smelled of desperation and was focusing all of my attention on not messing up. Because I was SO focused on my fears, I would mess up every single time. But that all changed in 2009, when I got a call from my agent about a recurring role on HBO's hit show *Entourage*.

It was then that I decided that instead of freaking out about it, which is what I always did, this time I would try something new: I'd attempt to have more fun than I've ever allowed myself to have in the audition room. The audition came a few days later, and I was definitely nervous. But instead of letting my nerves take over and spiral me into a bunch of crazy thoughts, I decided to breathe deeply and put my attention on my intention—which was to have fun.

Minutes before it was my turn to go in and audition, I acknowledged the nerves but chose to focus on FUN. A few moments later, I heard, "Preston, you're up," and I went in the room, introduced myself, took a deep breath, and gave it my all. When I got to my car, I released a huge laugh because the process was so incredibly fun. It wasn't a ten-out-of-ten audition as far as my acting goes, but I was present to the energy of the room. THIS was why I got into acting in the first place: to play, to experience, and to dance in my imagination.

Feeling the buzz of that audition, I thought how ridiculous it was that I had been doing anything other than simply having fun. I drove home that day with a sense of enormous accomplishment. Whether I booked the job or not, I felt like I had done my job for the first time since I'd been acting in LA.

The next day my agent called screaming! She said I had done so well that they wanted to book me on the spot, and there was no need for a callback (which rarely happens in that business). This was the beginning of my truly understanding that WHERE ATTENTION GOES, ENERGY FLOWS. Over the next two years, I booked countless movies, television shows, and commercials, all due largely to my shift in attention. I was on fire, and I knew that if I kept focusing on a positive intention and outcome, I would continue to get incredible results.

Confucius said, "He who says he can, and he who says he can't, are both usually right." Basically this means that your mind will always find a way to prove you right; that whatever you're predominantly putting your thoughts on, the universe will match in your reality. Loving louder is about understanding that you're the painter, the artist, the photographer, or the sculptor of your own life; and that no matter what happens, you have the POWER to shift your life by shifting where and what you put your attention on. So what would you like to bring more of into your world today?

# #LoveLouderChallenge

What's one area of your life that you continue to experience negative results in? It could be that you tend to attract relationships that don't work, you have a hard time finding or keeping work, or you just can't seem to catch a break. Knowing that what we focus on, we get more of, what subconscious thoughts do you believe have attracted these circumstances in your life? Now, what positive counter-thoughts could you focus on that would begin to attract a new set of circumstances?

# 20

# Powerful Questions Call for Powerful Answers

*I*f you are not inspired or motivated by the life you're living, it may be because you're not asking yourself high-quality questions. I've found that people who consistently ask empowering questions consistently live empowered lives, and those who struggle through life looking for inspiration are consistently asking uninspiring questions. Quality questions create a quality life.

Loving louder is about consciously asking questions that push us forward, challenging us to see through a different lens.

When I became aware of the questions I was asking myself, I noticed how low they were in quality and how they affected my reality. Before my feet hit the ground in the morning, I was already thinking thoughts like "What fires do I need to put out today?" I'd find myself in stores wondering why I always chose the line with the one person who takes forever. And some of my most popular questions to myself were "What's wrong with me?" "What if I can't do it?" "Am I smart enough to pull this off?"

Sound familiar? Our minds work a lot like a Google search. Whenever you ask a question, out loud or in your mind, your mental computer responds with an answer based on the key words you used. For instance, a question like "What's wrong with me?" sends your mental computer on a search for everything it perceives to be wrong with you. Why? Because you presented it with a disempowering question and it gave you the answers you asked for. You can ask questions that reinforce negativity, pessimism, and a victim mentality or questions that empower, energize, and replenish that untapped well of positivity inside of you, which creates opportunity and possibility. The following questions are designed to amplify your awareness and support you in loving louder.

## MORNING QUESTIONS

What am I most grateful for right now?

Whom do I absolutely love? Who loves the crap out of me?

What am I most excited about in my life right now?

## MIDDAY QUESTIONS

What am I committed to right now?

What's my intention for this moment?

What am I most proud of in my life right now?

## END-OF-THE-DAY QUESTIONS

How did whatever I experienced today (whether positive or negative) serve me?

What worked and what didn't work today, and how can I improve?

## TOUGH SITUATION QUESTIONS

What is my sight now allowing me to see?

What good is here that I presently cannot see?

What would love do now?

What's the highest choice in this moment?

Will this matter three years from now?

Am I taking this too seriously?

Am I present right now?

If you really want to amplify your life, make this part of your daily routine and post these questions where you can see them. We're empowered or disempowered by the quality of questions we ask ourselves on a daily basis. Get specific—vague requests produce vague results. By asking these questions and others like them, you'll open up your capacity to love louder, bringing more excitement, joy, harmony, and gratitude into your life.

# Love
will find a way;
EVERYTHING ELSE WILL FIND AN EXCUSE.

# 21

# BECOMING VERSUS REVEALING

$O$ver a century ago, a dude named Russell Conwell was famous for delivering a lecture in which he encouraged people to find the "acres of diamonds" in their own backyards. In 1870, Conwell went on a trip along the Tigris River, in present-day Iraq, hiring a guide who would take him to the Persian Gulf. These river guides were known to tell many elaborate stories, but the story this particular guide told, Conwell said, changed his life forever.

At the heart of the book *Acres of Diamonds* by Russell Conwell was a parable that in summary goes like this:

*The story is about a man named Ali Hafed who was very happy with his life. He was a rich man because he had everything he needed: his farm, his beautiful family, and money. Then one day a priest who was visiting Ali told him about diamonds in a far-off land that were worth a lot of money. The priest explained that if he had one of these rare diamonds he could have not just one farm, but many; and be set for generations to come.*

*Intrigued by the diamonds and how much they were worth, Ali went to bed that night a poor man. He had not lost anything, but he was poor because what he had was no longer enough. In a moment, he shifted his focus from all that he felt blessed to have, to all that he didn't yet possess.*

*So soon after that day, Ali sold his farm, left his family, and traveled the world searching for the rare diamonds. He traveled for years but he couldn't find them. His health and his wealth declined, and he felt like a failure. His feelings overwhelmed him and he threw himself into the ocean—knowing he could not swim—and drowned.*

*Meanwhile the man who had purchased Ali's farm saw a sparkling stone in a stream cutting through his land. He picked it up and put it on his mantel, not thinking anything of it. When the priest came by a few days later and asked him where he got this diamond, the man explained that it was just a rock and there were many on the land. It turns out that rock, and all the others on Ali's old land, were diamonds. In fact, after digging all over the land the two men found acres of diamonds. According to the story, these diamonds were to be the famous diamonds of Golconda, one of the biggest diamond mines in the world.*

So what does this mean for us? It means that we have to stop looking elsewhere for the diamonds. It means the gems are already here, but sometimes we get blinded by what we think they're supposed to look like. I hear so many people ask, "How do I become rich?" "How do I become more attractive?" "How can I become a better person?" These questions are ultimately a trap. Because we end up chasing an elusive carrot that we never seem to get.

*The question is not about becoming, the question is about revealing.* When we concentrate on having to become something, we miss the brilliance of who we already are. When we're looking in our neighbors' yard, noticing what they have, we miss the beauty of the yard that we're standing in. We need to tend to the ground we're standing on before charging off in search of greener pastures. You're perfect right here, right now. You're a beauty right here, right now. You don't need to *have* anything else to *BE* amazing. The diamonds are already here, because they are within you.

It's not about becoming, it is about revealing—revealing what's already there, hidden under your scars and psychological wounds. Today you get to sidestep your stories and reveal who you really are, which is pure love.

# #LoveLouderChallenge

Stop right now and list off ten things that are amazing about YOU. Do not go anywhere or do anything until you have at least ten. Then repeat this mantra, allowing it to sink into your emotions, five times a week: "I AM THE DIAMONDS."

# 22

# Give Up to Go Up:

## The Power of Sacrifice

*E*levation requires separation, and at the heart of loving louder is sacrifice. It requires letting go of unhealthy habits, shedding certain relationships, and sacrificing small thinking and excuses. It's been said that if you want something you've never had, you have to do something you've never done. And on August 18, 2012, I finally began to truly embody what that means.

After years of hangovers and blurry nights, I made the decision to sacrifice drinking alcohol until further notice. The decision was based on giving up my short-term *perceived* pleasure for my long-term happiness and well-being. I looked at how I felt when I was drinking and concluded that it wasn't having any positive effects on me; therefore it had to go. I got tired of talking about living my best life and then doing things that I knew weren't in alignment with that.

Aristotle has said, "We are what we repeatedly do. Excellence, then, is not an act, but a habit."

Many people have grand dreams but aren't willing to sacrifice what it takes to achieve them. They have poor habits, and those habits keep them stuck. We can't create more love in our lives until we have the courage to sacrifice those habits that aren't serving us. Most of the habits that keep us from loving louder are done without the conscious awareness that they're being done.

For years, I watched TV shows that centered on crime and violence, never making the correlation between watching the shows and fearing that something bad was going to happen to me or someone I loved. It wasn't until I sacrificed the habit of negative TV that I understood that it was one of the main things stopping me from seeing love everywhere I went.

We all have something or someone we know isn't serving our highest growth or good. Whether it's a friend who's constantly negative, gossiping and complaining about life, or a social media app that you find yourself checking every five minutes—if it isn't serving you, it has to go. Loving louder is about reevaluating what's important, eliminating those things that are in the way, and replacing them with new, healthy habits.

Sacrifice will look different for each one of us; only you know what you need to give up to go up. Some have to give up aspects of their personal lives; others need to let go of certain hobbies. The circumstances will be different from person to person, but the principle of sacrifice remains. Are you willing to miss the concert to work on your dream? Are you willing to sign off social media to ensure that you accomplish your vision? Sacrifice may not always be easy, but it is sometimes necessary for us to get to that next level.

# #LoveLouderChallenge

Make a list of everything you know isn't serving you. No matter how crazy it may sound, even if it's a family member, a job, or a favorite pastime, write it down. Then circle the three that you least want to give up. Yup, you're onto me. Now choose one of those three and create a strategy for removing that/them from your life, for now.

# DON'T FORGET

# to dance!

## Motion creates emotion.

# 23
# Just Say No

*J*ust because you're not busy doesn't mean you're available.

Your actions speak a lot louder than your words, and they show what you are truly committed to. If you're doing things that you don't want to do out of a feeling of obligation, then saying yes to someone actually means you're saying no to yourself. Learning to own your no is about setting healthy boundaries, committing to your needs and desires, and owning your life.

Learning to say no was one of the most challenging

and most rewarding things I've ever taken on. Deep in my subconscious, I had a story that I had to say yes to everything that was offered to me, that saying no was somehow rude and selfish. I was so enmeshed in this story that I felt pressured to do all kinds of things that I didn't want to do. I was saying yes to the good and okay things so much that when the great things came along, I didn't have the energy or time for them because I was overbooked. That was until I learned the power of saying *NO* for the sake of my greater commitments.

When I got that I didn't need a reason other than self-care and personal sanity, my life changed drastically. I went on a journey to discover my "burning YES," as Stephen Covey calls it, committing myself to prioritizing those FIRST in my life. Once I got clear on my priorities, I began to say no to everything that didn't bring me closer to my commitments.

It's about deciding what matters the most and having the audacity, from a place of love, to unapologetically say no. The first step in owning your NO is getting clear on your YES.

Exploring what you stand for, what burns deep in your gut, and who you choose to be on a daily basis will serve as your internal compass as you navigate the world. Even though it may seem tough to say no, remember that every time you say yes to someone or something that you don't truly want to do, you say no to yourself and your priorities.

Last—and this was a hard one for me to initially implement—it's okay to say no even if you've already said yes. You can always renegotiate your agreements with integrity while finding solutions that work for everyone. Take this book, for example. I agreed to have it in on a certain date, but as I dove deeper into the process, I realized that I was going to need to renegotiate that date. After a few emails and phone calls, my editor and I came to a date that felt doable for all parties involved. You'll only end up with bitterness if you agree to something out of obligation or fear. It's much more powerful to make a decision that feels right in your heart than to follow through with a decision just because you think you should.

# #LoveLouderChallenge

## Three Big Questions to Find Your Big YES

1. What most excites you about life? (For me, the answers would be empowering people to live authentic, loving lives; surfing; kissing my wife; and creating.)

2. What is one project, person, or activity that you wish you had more time for?

3. When I'm _____, I feel alive and on purpose.

Answer these questions and immediately begin to say no to everything that doesn't align with your answers. The key is to be loving and authentic, letting go of the need to overexplain or defend your decision.

You could say something like "This doesn't feel right for me at this moment," which is a perfectly valid reason. Or you could decline while reaffirming your commitment, which is a powerful stance with no wiggle room: "Thank you for thinking of me, but because I'm committed to _____, I'll have to decline." Don't fret. As you practice saying no, it will get easier (and you may even begin to like it!).

# 24

# Let It Flow:

## Harnessing the Power of Breathing

*M*ost of us suck at breathing. It's one of those things we do automatically, never having a second thought about it. Sure, we know that without it we would die, but there is so much more to our breath than that. Our breath, when done properly, is incredibly restorative. It can help rid us of worries and tensions and bring us back to our true nature, which is love. Conscious deep breathing is the key to amplifying physical, emotional, and spiritual well-being—softening, opening, and creating more space for love. The key to this type of conscious breathing is awareness.

Now, this may sound odd, but BREATHING is one of the most transformative things I've ever done. When I relearned how to breathe, it transformed my life, taking me everywhere from full belly, uncontrollable laughter to a flood of tears. Learning to breathe also supported me countless times in the midst of sticky situations, as it gave me perspective so that I could show up with more love in all areas of my life.

Turning up the volume and loving louder requires *conscious breathing*. It sounds so simple, but so many of us do it wrong; most of us are shallow chest breathers. We are taught to "suck it in" and to keep everything "contained." Breathing fully and freely is our birthright, and it's there for a good reason. Although we're all born knowing how to breathe, the hectic nature of our lives tends to lead to constricted breathing, making us feel as if we're running on fumes.

I've noticed that in stressful situations, the first thing that goes away is the breath. Whether we are at a scary movie, in the middle of a heated argument, or in the midst of something that requires our full attention, most of us stop breathing and clench our stomach and our jaw in preparation for an "attack."

When our breathing is short and rapid, our stress

hormones kick in. Back in the day, this was an indication to the body that "I am being chased by a saber-toothed tiger; I must run!" Today's stressors are more in the line of "I have to get this email out before my deadline" or "I'm pissed off at my friend." No matter what the stressors may be, they strain our system and drain us, leaving us feeling exhausted and depleted.

So when everything seems too much to handle or when you're stuck between a rock and a hard place, don't forget to breathe. The breath is there to remind you to come back to your center, ground yourself, and take a moment to gain perspective on what's actually happening. It's like a reset button, ready to restore us back to our default setting.

# #LoveLouderChallenge

Place one hand on your lower belly and take a slow, deep breath through your mouth, noticing your abdomen expanding as you inhale. As you exhale, blow out through your mouth again and feel your stomach contract. Repeat this three to five times today to get into the habit of conscious breathing.

# SLOW DOWN.

# 25
# MEDITATION

About five years ago on a plane to India, I read a line in what has now become my favorite book that changed my life. In *Conversations with God*, Neale Donald Walsch wrote: *"If you don't go within, you'll go without."* Shortly after I read this, I began a slow but methodical meditation practice that eventually turned into a daily practice.

Meditation is not reserved just for Buddhist monks or the "spiritual types." It's a practice any of us can do, no matter where we are or what we believe. It's not just about tapping into something deeper within ourselves; the practice of meditation has an insane number of health benefits. Some of the amazing side effects I experience are a more grounded and calm way of being, amazing insights that I can apply to my life, less stress, and a stronger immune system.

While I struggled with the "right way" to do it at first, I finally realized that there is no right or wrong way to meditate. There is no set amount of time; there are no hard rules about what to feel or how to sit or hold your hands. All that matters is that you begin. It's not what you do with your body but what you do with your mind that counts in meditation. It's about purposely going within and accepting whatever comes up and comes through in that space. Images and thoughts *will show up*, and that's okay. Through our practice, we learn to dissociate ourselves from those thoughts and simply watch as they pass by. Your body may experience some discomfort at first, and that's totally normal; with time you'll learn how to melt into your body and find a stillness that will carry you through.

# #LoveLouderChallenge

Today I challenge you to set aside five to ten minutes to find a quiet place and go within. Begin wherever you are and know that you will grow into your practice with commitment and persistence.

old, when my second-grade teacher would give us dead-lines for our in-classroom reading assignments. Although I wasn't aware of my dyslexia at the time, I knew some-thing was off. We were given three minutes to read two paragraphs, and like clockwork, as we neared the three-minute mark, the teacher would ask who needed more time. And in a moment of shame, I'd raise my hand while all the other kids looked and scoffed at me. As you probably guessed, the scoffs from my fellow classmates put a quick stop to my asking for more time. Because of my shame and fear, I didn't do well in school. I felt that I was constantly racing against the clock. It wasn't until 2005 that I came to acknowledge my rela-tionship with time and began to study how to better that relationship.

I discovered that time wasn't the issue, but how I was thinking about it was. When it came to time, I was making two big mistakes. First, I had the belief that time was always out of my control, and second, I was constantly overcommitting myself to try and make every-one happy. I was taking on too much and therefore scrambling to keep up with all my commitments, all the while holding firm to the victim mentality that time was against me. We've been taught that we can have it all, but as I mentioned earlier in this book, sometimes we have to give up to go up. So when we say we "don't have enough time," what we're really saying is "I don't know how to manage my time effectively."

Is all that we are doing on a daily basis really *that* important? Sure, we've got bills to pay and mouths to feed, but somehow in the hundred and sixty-eight hours we have in a week, we find time to watch TV, scroll through social media, and gossip with friends. We make time for so many unimportant things, all while complaining that there's not enough time in the day for our families, our dreams, or ourselves. We all have the same twenty-four hours in a day, and it is completely up to us to choose how we spend them. Loving louder is about viewing time as a tool. Just like any tool, it can be put to good use or totally forgotten about in our garage. But of course time can't be saved for later, stockpiled, or replaced like a hammer can. This tool called time must be utilized minute by minute, and once we use it, we can never get it back.

What I'm suggesting here is to be masterful with your time. How do you want to use it? Whom do you want to spend it with? What do you want to create in your minutes or hours of every day? Every decision we make costs us time, and it is indeed a precious resource. If we want to live extraordinary lives, we must become aware of how, with whom, and on what we spend our time.

# Ten years ago,

*I turned my head for a **moment** and it **became** my life.*

—David Whyte

We must be vigilant when it comes to the habits we produce around our time. I've seen, heard, and been the person who swears it's "just two more minutes," and those two minutes become the habits of our lives, destroying relationships, killing dreams, and sapping our vitality. The key to becoming masterful with time is to prioritize what's important first and then schedule in what you value so that you can manage it.

# #LoveLouderChallenge

Tonight make a plan for your day tomorrow. What will you feel amazing about accomplishing by the end of tomorrow? Maybe it's time with your loved ones with no technology, or maybe it's some solo time in silence or taking a few steps toward that big dream you have. Whatever is important to YOU, schedule it and make it happen.

# 27

# The Family Plan:

## How to Navigate Family

They say you can choose your friends, but you can't choose your family. They also say that life doesn't give you the people you want, but it gives you the people you need. Sometimes our relationships with family can be our most challenging, but know that they are here to grow you. What people said or did in the past is not who they are right now, in this moment. See people in the NOW and give them a chance to show up differently.

No, we can't change what happened, but we can

change how we view it. No one is perfect, and everyone's doing the best they can from where they currently are. When we hold our friends and family in *high regard*, they are more likely to respond from that same space. I don't know much, but what I do know is that when all is said and done, the only thing that matters is love. Every time any of my friends or family has ever been faced with anything potentially life threatening, whatever was a "problem" between us before goes out the window, and we come back to LOVE immediately. The key is to not wait until those you care about are sick or injured to reach out and to see them in their greatness; the key is to be proactive about it so we don't miss our opportunity to heal what needs to be healed.

# #LoveLouderChallenge

Next time you get triggered by someone, ask yourself: What am I committed to creating here? What would this look like if I didn't take it personally? And what story do I have running that is no longer serving me?

# 28

# Your Vibe Attracts Your Tribe:

## Friend Request

*Tell me who your best friends are
and I will tell you who you are.*
—John Mason

You are who you spend the most time with. No matter how you slice it, the company you keep will propel and lift you or will suppress and destroy you. Some of the people you love the most and you have known the longest can be the most toxic relationships in your life. I'm not a proponent of getting rid of a friend for a new and shinier model, but I do think we all need to take inventory of what we want out of life and see if the people we spend most of our time with match up with that.

There was a time when some of my best friends started selling drugs and carrying guns. And while I loved them, the path that they were on didn't fit into my vision for my future. I saw myself doing more than simply sticking around the neighborhood, gangbanging, and chasing women. So I made a tough decision to separate myself from them. I spent less and less time hanging out and more time in the basketball gym, with people who were more aligned with what I was calling in.

I'll never forget one summer when I came back home from college. I drove over to where the old crew was hanging out in a friend's garage. I had really started to explore my self-expression in fashion, and I walked into a garage full of weed smoke and forty-ounce beers, wearing lavender skinny jeans, a ripped-up shirt, pink converse Chuck Taylors, and a studded belt. They all immediately began to laugh and make fun of my outfit, but I was so confident in myself and all that I had experienced leaving Harbor City that I laughed with them and began to explain my experiences in college. As the day went on, each one of them pulled me aside and asked me—and I'm getting emotional writing this—where they went wrong. They each noticed that while we all grew up together and came from the same beginnings, I traveled the world and had all these experiences that they could only dream about. It pained me and gave me a profound sense of pride, all at the same time. The pride came from knowing that I was brave enough to separate myself from them and surround myself with people who challenged my thinking and who saw life outside of the box drawn for us. The pain came because I felt as if I had left them behind, and because I didn't know how I could possibly bring them with me.

You don't need to get rid of those friends completely, but if you feel drained every time you're around them, this is an indicator that the relationship is not serving you. When you hang with complainers, pessimists, and people who operate from a victim mentality, it makes it super hard for you to be anything other than that; it's human nature to want to fit in.

If you're calling in an extraordinary life, steer clear of small thinkers with small plans and upgrade your group of friends to people who share a similar vision of the world. Surround yourself with people who think big and put actions behind their thoughts. These are the people who will support your highest growth and challenge you to step further into what's possible for your life.

If you don't know anyone who's interested in the stuff you are, go out and find them. The beautiful thing about the Internet is, it's easy to find people who like the same stuff as you.

And when you do find your tribe, make sure you let them know how much you appreciate them. We're social beings, we need one another, and you can't put a price tag on a good friend. They are the ones walking in when everyone else is walking out. They are the ones who will be there with you through the good times and bad times. Through all the struggles, disagreements, and laughter (until you pee your pants), you create a bond that will keep on giving.

# #LoveLouderChallenge

Make a list of the five people you spend the most time with.

When you think of each person, what three things immediately come to mind? (Examples: he complains, he's funny, she's supportive, she's argumentative.)

Do you feel elevated or brought down after spending time with them?

Now make a list of five qualities you'd like your friends to have.

# STOP COMPARING YOUR JOURNEY

to anyone else's.

WHAT YOU CAME TO DO, BE, AND HAVE

is unique to you.

# 29

# Never-Never Land:

## Get Off Fantasy Island

Most of us hold ourselves to unattainable "fantasy" standards that we can never live up to. If we spend countless hours in a gym trying to get a perfect body like the airbrushed models in the magazines, always want to have the right answer, hope never to make a mistake, or try to match up to some religious doctrine, we are setting ourselves up for a life of disappointment. We punish ourselves for not having it all together, as if that's even possible. Loving louder is about taking a look at the fantasy standards we've been holding ourselves to and creating new, healthier ones that match our soul signature.

I discovered this about myself when, in a heated argument with my best friend years ago, he pointed out how hard it was for me to admit when I was wrong. He said that I always found a way to turn it around and never take full responsibility. After I picked my ego up off the ground, it hit me like a ton of bricks—he was right. You see, from an early age I had the fantasy standard that "real men" always had to have it together. All the men I idolized on film and television were gun-toting, self-assured manly men who always seemed to have the right answer. So even when I realized I didn't have it all together or have the right answers, I pretended that I did in order to try and live up to that standard. When I began to catch myself trying to meet this fantasy standard, it drastically transformed my life. I felt a sense of freedom in knowing that I *didn't* have to have it all together and that I was and always will be a work in progress. As I started living from this way of being, I began to see that a lot of other men try to meet this particular fantasy standard as well, whether it's not asking for directions when we're lost or expecting ourselves to be the sole provider for our family or to always be emotionally strong even when we may be heartbroken.

Women are certainly not excluded when it comes to having fantasy standards. From an early age, women are consciously and unconsciously taught to live up to a societal standard of what beautiful is. They think that if they don't have a small waist, curves in all the right places, perfect skin, and full lips, they're not beautiful. From TV commercials to billboards, the media is constantly feeding them a story about how they're not enough.

Loving louder is about being authentically YOU. Trying to fix yourself based on a fantasy standard society has set and you have bought into is a task you'll never complete, because there is nothing to fix. You are perfect, whole, and complete, but you're not finished. Yes, you have work to do, but you're not lacking anything. Everything you are is more than enough. There is nothing to fix, because that would imply that you were broken; instead you're simply bettering your best.

Give yourself a break and release yourself from the shackles of comparison and fantasy standards. We all came here to be us and nobody else. You can't fail—if you're living, you're already winning. Let that land: *If you're living, you're already winning.* Honor the gift that you are by recasting or letting go of the standards that have been holding you hostage.

# #LoveLouderChallenge

Make a list of the fantasy standards you hold yourself to. Is it that you won't be happy until you have the perfect body? Or the perfect partner? Or maybe it's having the house always immaculate, even if you've got toddlers running around. What are you holding yourself to that is holding your happiness hostage?

# AMPLIFY YOUR LOVE, amplify YOUR LIFE.

# 30

# CHILDLIKE, NOT CHILDISH:

## FEED YOUR INNER CHILD

When I was nine, my buddies and I would make homemade Molotov cocktails that consisted of urine, mud, ketchup, rocks from my mom's garden, and whatever else we could take from the surrounding area. Once we had a good number of them made, we would ride around the neighborhood throwing them at people's garages and biking away as fast as possible. Now, while

I don't condone my pre-adolescent mischief, I do look back at that with a smile, because while our actions may have been irresponsible and mean, we were playing and using our imaginations to create. It was as if time stopped when we would get into these playful zones, and the rest of the world would melt away. It's my belief that play is an essential element in living a fulfilled and joyful life. But somewhere in the journey toward becoming an adult we lose our playfulness, and with it we lose a sense of vitality.

Underneath all that adult seriousness is your inner child, champing at the bit to get wild and play again. Life is not as serious as we make it out to be with our manners, rules, and social protocol. Kids don't give a flying pig knuckle about manners and being politically correct. (And yes, I said pig knuckle!) Kids play, laugh, dance, scream, cry, and joke like champions. They own the now, and while we shush them and do our best to teach them how to be upstanding citizens, I think there's a bright-eyed, bushy-tailed innocent love nugget in all of us, wanting to connect to that innate freedom through play.

No matter what you do in the world, no matter what your age, we ALL need to enjoy this life to the best of our ability. So put down that phone and go do something fun . . . you owe it to your inner child.

# #LoveLouderChallenge

Make a list of everything you can imagine would be fun to experience (and I mean everything!). This doesn't mean you'll be able to do it all, but the fun starts with the imagination. I'll give you a few examples from my list of things I either do on a regular basis or aspire to do more of.

Skip

Surf

Climb trees

Have tickle wars with my wife

Spark a conversation with a stranger

Dance in my underwear

Spin around until I get dizzy

Eat coconut ice cream while sitting in the park

Play Scrabble with my best friend

Make up code words with my best friend

You get it. Now, after you have no fewer than twenty ideas, I want you to share the three things you're committed to doing this week with a friend and challenge him or her to do the same. Deal?

# #LoveLouderChallenge

Make a list of everything you can imagine would be fun to experience (and I mean everything!). This doesn't mean you'll be able to do it all, but the fun starts with the imagination. I'll give you a few examples from my list of things I either do on a regular basis or aspire to do more of.

Skip

Surf

Climb trees

Have tickle wars with my wife

Spark a conversation with a stranger

Dance in my underwear

Spin around until I get dizzy

Eat coconut ice cream while sitting in the park

Play Scrabble with my best friend

Make up code words with my best friend

You get it. Now, after you have no fewer than twenty ideas, I want you to share the three things you're committed to doing this week with a friend and challenge him or her to do the same. Deal?

# 31

# When Nature Calls, Go Outside and Play

While I love a good touch screen in the palm of my hand, there is nothing like being in the palm of nature to remind us of how vast, powerful, and majestic our planet is.

I spend as much time as possible surfing in Malibu, California, at Surfrider Beach. While I didn't have the vocabulary or understanding twelve years ago of why it filled me up every time I stepped into nature, surfing has been one of the biggest factors for my internal happiness and all-around health. There is something about connecting with nature that fuels creativity and boosts vitality for life.

We can get so caught up in our busy schedules, work, and the seemingly endless options on the Internet and television all jockeying for our attention that we end up forgetting the healing and creative power of nature. Nature is and always will be the best show on earth. You can look up at the night sky or at a raging waterfall; listen to the thundering roar of the ocean waves; be amazed by the sheer brilliance of a colony of ants, the magic of a caterpillar turning into a butterfly, or the audacity of a lion hunting buffalo; or be thrilled by the first snowfall in New York City. Nature has a way of reminding us of how small we really are and yet how we are a piece of the larger whole. We too are part of nature, and our being calls to be surrounded by it. But in this fast-paced world, we've separated ourselves from nature, and it's time we get back to it. Loving louder is about connecting back to the source and breathing in all its beauty.

We all need time in nature, time to be recharged by the trees, baptized by the seas, suffused by the fragrance of the flowers, and reenergized by the air. (Unless you live in a smog-filled urban jungle, and then at that point you're better off inside. . . . I'm joking!) I grew up in and continue to live in the concrete jungles of LA, and I still find a way to connect with the natural world. Our planet is alive, aware, and awake, and when we tap into its power by communing with it, we travel along the royal road to loving louder.

# #LoveLouderChallenge

Go outside!

Whether it's a ten-minute morning walk around the block, a midnight stroll after work, a hike in your local forest, or a swim in the nearest body of water, exercising outdoors instead of going to the gym, or having lunch on the patio instead of inside, get out a minimum of three times a week to experience the beauty of our spinning blue dot called Earth.

# 32

# DEFINE IT, THEN DESIGN IT

*Loving louder is about living life by design and not default.*

Too many people are chasing money instead of passion; living the lives their parents or society has mapped out for them, instead of carving out their own paths and designing a life that feels good to them.

If you're like me, you grew up hearing from well-meaning parents, teachers, grandparents, and school counselors that "You have to get good grades so you can get into a good college and then get a good job." And if you're anything like me, you bought this hook, line, and sinker. Why? Because you had no other point of reference of another way. You trusted their advice even if it didn't seem all that important to you at the time. No knock against education and living the dream, but for me and many others, that way of living doesn't mesh with who we are.

In my second year of graduate school, I realized that I wasn't in school because I wanted to be. I was in school because I was afraid of not amounting to anything worthy by society's standards. In this epiphany, I realized that those unwritten rules for success were true for my parents and the time they lived in, but such rules were no longer true for me and many others.

When it comes right down to it, *real* success, not the standardized ideal of it, looks different for everyone. These discoveries pushed me to challenge all the conventional thinking I was subscribing to and redefine success on my terms.

# Those who *live* *extraordinary lives* **define** and **design** success on **their** *terms.*

I define success as creating an impact on the world, leaving it better than I found it. While success used to be defined by finite things (a certain job title, a given amount of money in my bank account, a brand-name car, or a high-end zip code), I now define my life as successful when I'm in the journey of what makes me happy.

Those who live extraordinary lives of joy and purpose usually didn't set out to be rich and powerful; instead, they defined success by their terms and set out to design a life that aligned with what they truly cared about. That commitment to their heart's calling creates a path of joy, bliss, and fulfillment, no matter what it looks like to the outside world.

# #LoveLouderChallenge

What is success on your terms?

Some examples would be being a good mom, being healthy, creating art, going to concerts once a month, being able to work from home, and so forth. Make a list and get to work on designing it.

# 33

# There Is No Elevator to Success; We All Have to Take the Stairs

*O*nce you have defined what success looks like for you and have begun to design it, next comes the work. There's no substitute for hard work; we all have to roll up our sleeves and take the stairs to get to that floor we're going after.

The Roman philosopher Seneca once said, "Luck is what happens when preparation meets opportunity."

The preparation is the work, and the opportunity will find us when we are truly ready to work and make it ours.

While some get caught up in wishful thinking, visualizations, and acting as if they already have it, the one thing that glues the whole process together is putting in the elbow grease. A gardener can't just wish for a beautiful garden and one suddenly appears; she has to choose the seed, pick the place, clear the ground, dig the holes, plant the seed, water it, add mulch, and repeat these steps over and over again if she wants to experience that beautiful healthy garden in the flesh. Similarly, if you want to live a full, adventurous, abundant, joy-filled, and loving life, it's going to take work. Trust that there will be setbacks and temporary bumps along the journey, but they're nature's way of strengthening us to be ready for what it is we're working toward.

Hard work by itself is a powerful tool, but what really excites me is who you become in the process of doing the work. Every time you work through something that you initially thought was impossible, it builds character, increases self-respect, adds meaning, and solidifies new habits. It creates a new version of you to lean back on, knowing that anything is possible with enough faith, patience, and perseverance.

So instead of looking for shortcuts and avoiding the work, it's time to work toward your dream . . . full steam ahead. There is no elevator to loving louder; we all have to take the stairs.

# #LoveLouderAffirmation

I will work for it more than I hope for it.

You are perfect, whole, and complete,

# BUT YOU'RE NOT FINISHED.

# Afterword

lthough this may be the end of the book, it's not the end of your journey. Feel free to reread certain passages or the whole book so you absorb the principles and make them work for you. Rest assured, challenges will always come up, but you can use the tools and insights in this book to overcome them. Trust in the journey of life, knowing that your victories, your defeats, your joy, and your sadness are all part of the process.

You've been given a dream, a mission, a vision, and you need to get out of your own way to fulfill it. Life is like a dance party: Your job is to stay in rhythm with whatever song that's playing at the time. And if and when you fall out of rhythm—and we all do—turn your stumble into a new move and continue with ease.

Things won't change unless you do, but you don't have to have it all figured out. You just have to be willing to be vulnerable and open to change with the beat. I am, we are #LovesVoice.

# ACKNOWLEDGMENTS

My deep appreciation goes to the people who made this book possible. At Simon & Schuster, Michele Martin and Kathryn Huck for your tireless work and dedication to bringing this message to the masses. To everyone on my Facebook, YouTube, and Instagram pages who day in and day out send me encouragement and unwavering support. To my ATL family, particularly Bruce Cryer, Freeman Michaels, Barnet Bain, and Scott Coady for believing in me. Many thanks to Dr. Michael Bernard Beckwith for your direct and indirect mentorship. To my wife, Alexi Panos: your love warms my heart and makes everything worth it. Finally, special thanks to my unborn children and their children for being the inspiration for why I work so hard on being the best version of me. I hope that this book does you proud.

# About the Author

Preston Smiles is an internationally recognized next-generation thought leader and has a dedicated following on his YouTube channel. Preston has been featured in *LA Weekly, Los Angeles Magazine,* and *Origin* magazine, is a regular contributor to Huffington Post, The Daily Love, Good Guy Swag, and has appeared on top podcasts such as *The School of Greatness* and *Addicted2Success.* He has won *Elixir Magazine*'s Millennial Mentor Award and is one of the youngest members of ATL (Association of Transformational Leaders), founded by Jack Canfield. As a cofounder of both The Love Mob and The Bridge Method, a twelve-week online personal development program, Preston is no stranger to what it takes to live a life of love.